THE LI
ICE
TIPS

ANDREW LANGLEY

THE LITTLE BOOK OF ICE CREAM TIPS

ANDREW LANGLEY

A.
Absolute Press

First published in Great Britain in 2012 by
Absolute Press, an imprint of Bloomsbury Publishing Plc
Scarborough House, 29 James Street West
Bath BA1 2BT, England
Phone +44 (0)1225 316013 **Fax** +44 (0)1225 445836
E-mail info@absolutepress.co.uk
Web www.absolutepress.co.uk

A catalogue record of this book is available from the British Library
ISBN 13: 9781906650445
Printed and bound in Malta on behalf of Latitude Press

Bloomsbury Publishing Plc
50 Bedford Square, London WC1B 3DP | www.bloomsbury.com

'My advice to you is not to inquire why or whither, but just enjoy your ice cream while it's on your plate. That's my philosophy.'

Thornton Wilder (1897–1975),
US playwright and novelist

1

Ice cream has three elements.

The first is water, in the form of ice crystals. The second is fat, in the form of concentrated cream left when the water freezes. The third is air, distributed through the ice cream in tiny pockets by the mixing process. Getting the balance of these elements right is the secret of good ice cream.

2

Make your ice cream at the last feasible moment

– the same day as serving if you can.
It needs to taste as fresh and zingy as possible. Ices (including sorbets) which have been stored too long in the freezer tend to lose their sharpness. Store home-made stuff for a week at most.

3

Transfer the ice cream from the freezer to the fridge

at least one hour before serving. If it's too cold, it will be hard to dish out, and will leave the tongue numb and maybe scorched. It will also become smoother in texture as the water crystals begin to melt.

4

Store ice cream at the lowest possible temperature.

That means no higher than somewhere between -16° and -20°C (around 0°F). The intense cold keeps the ice cream properly frozen and prevents the ice crystals from thawing (even slightly). Thawed and re-frozen crystals tend to grow, thus ruining the smooth texture.

5

When you've finished serving,

put the ice cream back into the freezer as soon as possible.

If the ice cream melts, then either eat it up or throw it away. Avoid re-freezing melted ice cream – it's the safest option.

6

In the freezer, **always keep ice cream containers tightly sealed.**

This stops them from picking up odours from other foods. It's also wise to cover the surface of the ice cream in cling film, to prevent it being dried out by the chilled air.

7

Making your own ice cream: by hand or by machine?

Both have advantages. There is cost – good-quality ice cream makers with built-in freezers are expensive, while your hands come free. However, machine-made ice cream is definitely creamer and smoother than hand-made.

8

Vanilla ice cream – made by hand – is the one basic recipe you need.

Briefly boil 600ml (1 pint) of single cream with a dash of vanilla essence. Whisk 6 egg yolks in a bowl, then slowly stir in the cream plus 75g (3oz) of sugar. Heat very gently until it thickens. When cool, fold in some double cream. Freeze, stirring several times.

9

It is vital to

stir your ice cream before it has frozen completely. This breaks up ice crystals and gives a smooth consistency. Chill the mixture in the fridge for 2 hours, then move to the freezer for 30 minutes. Take out, stir and replace for another 30 minutes. Repeat twice more. (Or, of course, use a machine.)

10

Remember that any

ice cream which contains alcohol

(or a lot of sugar)

requires special attention. For a start, it will take longer to freeze than an ordinary ice. And, by logical extension, it will also begin to thaw more rapidly once out of the freezer.

11

The **soft smooth** texture of **ice cream goes perfectly with** something **crisp or crunchy.**

Cornets and wafers spring to mind, of course, but many other small sweet biscuits will add a more intriguing touch. *Langues de chat*, macaroons, amaretti or Italian *biscotti di Prato* would be perfect.

12

Here's the **simplest and quickest chocolate ice cream ever.**

Gently melt and stir together 170g (6oz) of good dark chocolate (at least 60% cocoa), 2 tablespoons of dark sugar and a carton of double cream. When cooled, mix in 450g (1lb) of custard (tinned or home-made). Freeze, stirring several times before solid.

13

Making a basic fruit sorbet is another

quick and straightforward

operation. For

lemon sorbet,

grate the zest from 4 lemons, then squeeze out the juice. Briefly boil 300ml ($^1/_2$ pint) water with 220g (8oz) sugar, add the zest and leave to cool. Stir in the lemon juice, strain and freeze, stirring a couple of times.

14

Granita is a southern **Italian** take on the **sorbet** (originally made with the snows from Mount Etna). The classic, naturally, is

coffee granita.

Make a water/sugar syrup as in 12, then stir in 220g (8 fl oz) exceedingly strongly brewed high-roast coffee. Cool and freeze, stirring to get a smooth consistency. Serve with cream.

15

Whole vanilla pods

bring more

intensity and flavour

to your ice creams than mere vanilla essence. Infuse them in the milk or cream you're using. Better still, slit the pods carefully and remove the seeds. These can be added to the mixture before the first freezing.

16

Sounds obvious perhaps, but if you're making

ice cream with fresh fruit, always purée the fruit first

(though cooking is usually unnecessary). This way, it will blend in with the custard. Whole fruits – even tiddlers like blueberries – contain a lot of water and will freeze as hard as lead shot.

17

Spice up your chocolate ice cream with chilli.

Steep 2 dried chiilies in 300ml (10 fl oz) heated milk for 30 minutes.Remove the chillies, reheat the milk and melt into it broken bar of good white chocolate. Stir this in with 4 beaten egg yolks and 50g (1¾ oz) sugar. Heat gently until thicker, then fold in double cream and freeze.

18

For an express ice,

freeze yoghurt with bananas.
Tip a tub of good Greek (drained) yoghurt into a bowl and whisk in 125g ($4\frac{1}{2}$oz) sugar. Mash 2 ripe bananas and mix them in. Chill and finish off in a machine, or simply freeze, stirring a few times before it gets solid.

19

Simplicity is the key to yoghurt ices.

It needs little preparation before freezing (heating should be avoided, as this makes it curdle). However, you can make the ice lighter by whisking in a couple of egg whites. Or you can make it even more sumptuous by whizzing in some double cream.

20

Ice cream machines come in two main forms.

The most convenient to use is the all-in-one automatic machine with its own freezer unit. It is also much the most expensive and bulky. The simpler and cheaper machine has a detachable bowl for chilling in the freezer. But it's more fiddley.

21

Use only plastic or wooden utensils when you're making ice cream with a machine. Metal spoons and spatulas can easily scratch or dent the soft alloy surface of the freezing bowl.

22

Experiment with your sorbet flavourings.

Unusual and exotic ingredients can produce sensational (or at least interesting) effects. Among the best are jasmine flowers, scented geranium leaves, mulberries, medlars, wild strawberries, calvados and cinnamon.

23

Classic ice cream sauce #1: butterscotch.

Heat 50g (1¾oz) unsalted butter gently with the same amount of brown sugar and 2 tablespoons syrup. Boil until it starts to thicken and leave to cool for 5 minutes. Then stir in 125ml (4fl oz) full-cream milk. Serve when still warmish.

24

Sicilian ice cream, in general, has a low fat content

because it contains less cream.
Heat milk and sugar as before, then add 4 tablespoons of cornflour to every litre of liquid. When cool, add 225g (8oz) of ground almonds, hazelnuts or pistachios according to taste. Freeze, stirring frequently.

25

The greatest Persian ice cream

depends on the availability of salep, or powdered orchid root. Lucky enough to find a supplier? Then beat together 450ml (1 pint) milk with 250g (8 ounces) sugar and a dash of rosewater. Stir in a teaspoon of salep and some double cream if you want. Freeze, stirring frequently.

26

Classic ice cream sauce #2: chocolate.

The better the chocolate, the better the sauce. Melt together a broken bar of high-grade dark chocolate, 3 tablespoons of syrup, the juice of one orange, a small tub of single cream and a knob of butter. Stir, adding a dash of Cointreau, and serve.

27

If possible, **have two scoops for serving ice cream.** Put both in a bowl of hot water. Pull one out, scoop out a portion of ice cream (remember to use the sharp edge). Then return the first scoop to the water and pull out the second one to use. This way, you'll always have a warm scoop available.

28

Serve your ice cream in an ice bowl.

You need two plastic bowls – one slightly smaller than the other. Half fill the big bowl with cold water and put the other one inside it, leaving a fingerwidth gap. Weight the inner bowl with a can of beans and freeze overnight. Run under cold water and ease off the plastic bowls.

29

Tea and limes make an intriguing combination for a **sorbet.** Boil up a water and sugar syrup as in Tip #12, adding the zest from three limes. Brew (for a few minutes) a similar quantity of strong tea, using orange pekoe or lapsang souchong. Mix this with the syrup and the juice of the limes and freeze – stirring as usual.

30

Fruit compote perfectly complements a rich **vanilla ice cream.** Here's one with fresh figs and pomegranates. Scoop the flesh from two pomegranates, blend briefly, then strain the juice. Add the juice of half a lemon, two tablespoons of honey and 450g (1lb) of fresh figs, peeled and cut up. Chill for 3 hours then serve over the ice cream.

31

Sparkling wine
such as prosecco or cava
goes brilliantly with most fruit ice creams. For a change, try it with fruit sorbets, especially lemon or orange. Pop a scoop into a tall glass, then top up with the fizzy – taking care it doesn't froth up and overflow.

32

For something different, try ice kachang,

or 'red bean ice', a speciality of Malaysia. It's colourful, exotic and incredibly simple (if you can source the ingredients). Adorn a pile of shaved ice with colourful fruit syrups, sweet aduki bean paste and a topping of evaporated milk or ice cream. Weird and wonderful.

33

Classic ice cream sauce #3: rum and raisin.

Soak 50g ($1^3/_4$oz) of raisins in 4 tablespoons of rum for an hour. Boil up a syrup of 50g ($1^3/_4$oz) brown sugar, a cinnamon stick, a knob of butter and a splash of water. Cool and add raisins and rum, plus lemon zest and (optional) a dash of double cream.

34

Did you know that February 1st is **Baked Alaska** Day in the US? **Just three components are needed:** a sponge base, a lump of vanilla ice cream on top and on top of that an igloo shape of meringue (at least four egg whites and 225g of sugar whipped). Bake in a hot oven (230°C) for 4 minutes and eat. A miracle.

35

Get a smoother sorbet by freezing it first of all in a shallow baking tray. When it's hardish, take it out of the freezer and break it into pieces. Put the fragments in a food processor and whizz up along with a beaten egg white. Then pop it in a box and return to the freezer.

36

Prunes add a bit of **magic to creamy vanilla ice cream** – that is, if you stone them and soak them in armagnac or oloroso sherry for a day or two beforehand. When the ice cream is churned but not yet frozen, stir in the prunes and their alcohol. Then freeze.

37

Beer and ice cream?

Yes – they can go together brilliantly, but you must choose with care. Perhaps the most suitable is Belgian lambic (wild-yeast) beer flavoured with cherry or raspberries, which is just sweet enough. Pour some over a couple of scoops of vanilla or fruit ice cream and tuck in.

38

Sherbets

lie somewhere between sorbets and ice creams, being mostly ice with a bit of cream.

The golden rule

is to mix the main ingredients at the last moment before freezing. Lemon juice, milk and eggs will not stand for long without separating.

39

To make a basic **apricot sherbet,** whizz up 1kg (2lb) of peel and stoned fresh apricots (or a big can of apricots) with juice from half a lemon and 60g (2oz) of sugar. Then add two beaten egg whites and a dash of almond essence. Freeze in the usual manner, stirring frequently.

40

Classic ice cream sauce #4: Melba.

Wash and purée 450g (1lb) of raspberries, then sieve to get rid of the pips. Heat gently with 60g (2oz) of icing sugar and the juice of half a lemon. Optional extras include a splodge of redcurrant jelly and a tablespoon of arrowroot mixed with a little water. Perfect with vanilla ice cream.

41

Praline is the **ideal** companion **for a rich chocolate ice cream.** Boil up a syrup of 3 tablespoons of water and 110g (4oz) of sugar until it bubbles. Stir in 150g (5oz) of toasted almonds and tip the whole lot out onto a tray. When cool, break up the praline and whizz it in a blender. Stir in with the ice cream just before freezing.

42

Put a ripple in your ice cream.

The easiest way is to put the unfrozen ice cream into its tub after churning in the machine. Pour in a modest amount of your chosen fruit or sugary sauce, then stir it (very gently) into ripple patterns with the handle of a wooden spoon. Freeze.

43

Get your servings ready ahead of time.

Place your carefully-wrought scoops of ice cream on a tray covered with greaseproof paper. Then stick them back into the freezer until needed. This way, you have individual servings ready and waiting.

44

Add an extra touch of **class** by giving ice cream a **chocolate coating.** Prepare your ice cream scoops as in Tip #43. Melt a bar of good dark chocolate in a bowl. Take out the frozen scoops and roll them in the chocolate using a pair of spoons or forks. Return immediately to the freezer for 15 minutes.

45

Remove ice cream stains from the carpet

as soon as possible. If they've dried, first scrape away as much as you can with a knife. Then dab (rather than rub) a dilute mix of dishwasher soap onto the residue. This may take perseverance, but eventually it will be gone. Rinse the spot with clean water and blot dry.

46

To **get rid of ice cream stains on clothes or other laundry,**

soak it in cold water (never hot) as soon as possible. If it lingers, rub in some detergent and leave for 15 minutes. Then wash as normal in a machine at a low temperature.

47

Classic ice cream sauce #5: Irish coffee.

Boil up a thick syrup of 225g (8oz) sugar and 50ml (2fl oz) water. Make an espresso cupful (about 25ml or 1fl oz) of good strong coffee and stir that in. Cool a little and add a slug of Irish whiskey – Jameson or Powers for preference.

48

There are plenty of ways to **make dairy-free ice cream,** such as this simple one for vegan chocolate. Whizz up a litre (2 pints) of soy milk, 165g (6oz) of soy milk powder and a tablespoon of cider vinegar. Heat in a saucepan with 450g (1lb) of sugar, 110g (4oz) of cocoa powder and a pinch of salt. When syrupy, cool and freeze.

49

Use up that leftover Christmas pud – turn it into ice cream. In a big bowl, whip together a big tub of double cream, the same quantity of custard and a good slug of brandy. Put through the ice cream machine as usual and pour into a tub. Stir in at least 225g (8oz) crumbled Christmas cake and freeze.

50

Italians love and respect their ice cream. That's why they sometimes eat it drizzled with olive oil. It should be Italian vanilla ice cream, and the oil should be cold pressed extra virgin – both the best you can buy. A modest scattering of flaked sea salt rounds it off.

Andrew Langley

Andrew Langley is a knowledgeable food and drink writer. Among his formative influences he lists a season picking grapes in Bordeaux, several years of raising sheep and chickens in Wiltshire and two decades drinking his grandmother's tea. He has written books on a number of Scottish and Irish whisky distilleries and is the editor of the highly regarded anthology of the writings of the legendary Victorian chef Alexis Soyer.

THE LITTLE BOOK OF
BARBECUE
TIPS
ANDREW LANGLEY

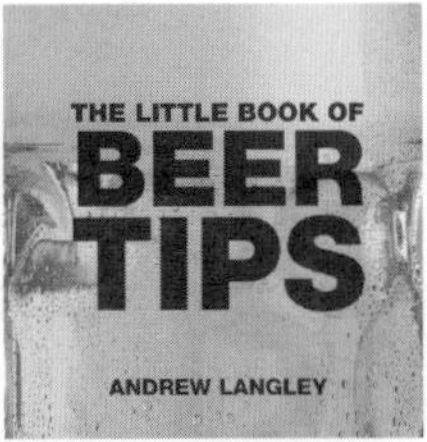
THE LITTLE BOOK OF
BEER
TIPS
ANDREW LANGLEY

THE LITTLE BOOK OF
HERB
TIPS
WILLIAM FORTT

THE LITTLE BOOK OF
POKER
TIPS
PETER FRENCH

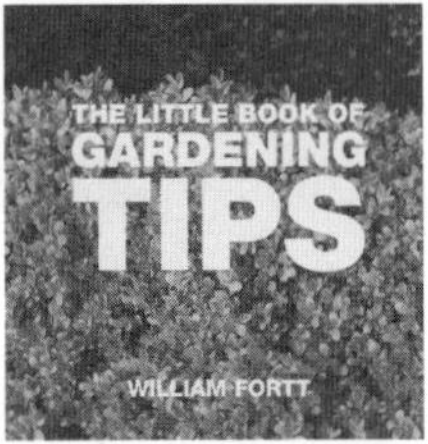
THE LITTLE BOOK OF
GARDENING
TIPS
WILLIAM FORTT

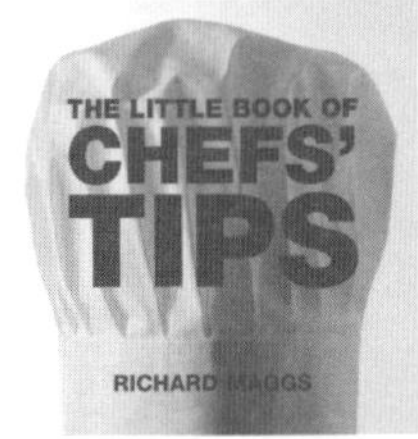
THE LITTLE BOOK OF
CHEFS'
TIPS
RICHARD MAGGS

THE LITTLE BOOK OF
SPICE
TIPS
ANDREW LANGLEY

THE LITTLE BOOK OF
GOLF
TIPS
PETER FRENCH

THE LITTLE BOOK OF
TIPS
SERIES

THE LITTLE BOOK OF
CHEESE
TIPS
ANDREW LANGLEY

THE LITTLE BOOK OF
WINE
TIPS
ANDREW LANGLEY
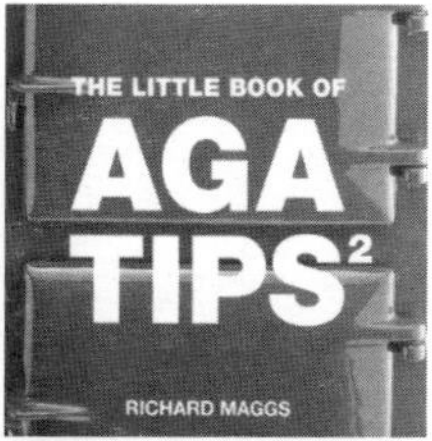
THE LITTLE BOOK OF
AGA
TIPS²
RICHARD MAGGS

THE LITTLE BOOK OF
COFFEE
TIPS
ANDREW LANGLEY

THE LITTLE BOOK OF
TEA
TIPS
ANDREW LANGLEY

THE LITTLE BOOK OF
AGA
TIPS³
RICHARD MAGGS

THE LITTLE BOOK OF
AGA
TIPS
RICHARD MAGGS

THE LITTLE BOOK OF
CHRISTMAS
AGA
TIPS
RICHARD MAGGS

THE LITTLE BOOK OF
RAYBURN
TIPS
RICHARD MAGGS

THE LITTLE BOOK OF
BRIDGE
TIPS
PETER FRENCH

THE LITTLE BOOK OF
CHESS
TIPS
PETER FRENCH

THE LITTLE BOOK OF
FISHING
TIPS
MICK DEVENISH

THE LITTLE BOOK OF
GREEN
TIPS
WILLIAM FORTT

THE LITTLE BOOK OF
KITTEN
TIPS
ANDREW LANGLEY

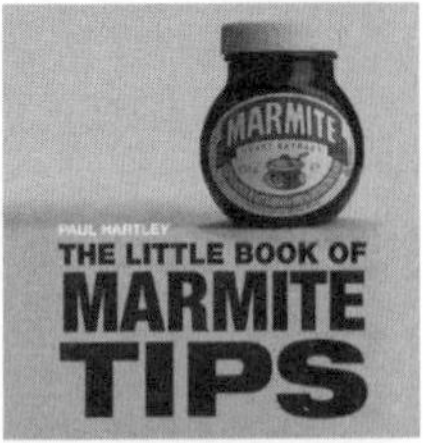
MARMITE
PAUL HARTLEY
THE LITTLE BOOK OF
MARMITE
TIPS

THE LITTLE BOOK OF
PUPPY
TIPS
ANDREW LANGLEY

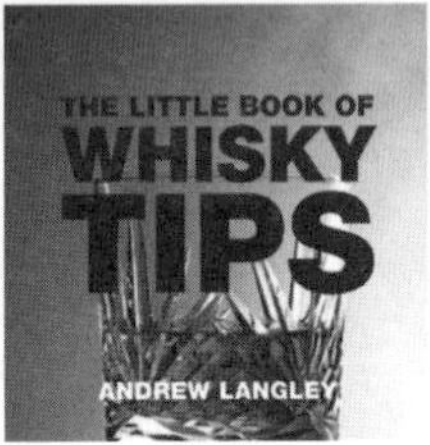
THE LITTLE BOOK OF
WHISKY
TIPS
ANDREW LANGLEY

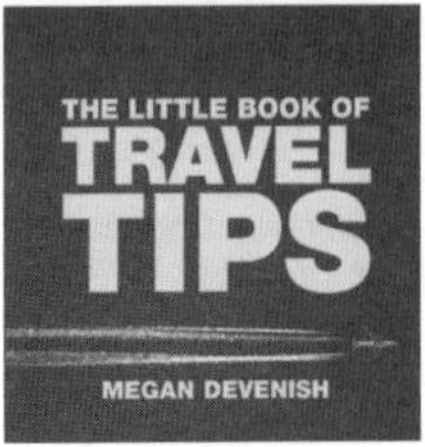
THE LITTLE BOOK OF
TRAVEL
TIPS
MEGAN DEVENISH

Little Books of Tips from Absolute Press

Aga Tips
Aga Tips 2
Aga Tips 3
Allotment Tips
Backgammon Tips
Barbecue Tips
Beer Tips
Bread Tips
Bridge Tips
Cake Baking Tips
Cake Decorating Tips
Cheese Tips
Chefs' Tips
Chess Tips
Chocolate Tips
Christmas Aga Tips
Chutney and Pickle Tips
Cocktail Tips
Coffee Tips
Cupcake Tips
Curry Tips
Fishing Tips
Fly Fishing Tips
Frugal Tips
Gardening Tips
Golf Tips
Green Tips
Grow Your Own Tips
Herb Tips
Houseplant Tips
Ice Cream Tips
Jam Tips
Kitten Tips
Macaroon Tips
Marmite Tips
Olive Oil Tips
Pasta Tips
Poker Tips
Puppy Tips
Rayburn Tips
Spice Tips
Tea Tips
Travel Tips
Whisky Tips
Wine Tips
Vinegar Tips